BRITISH MUSEUM

by the same author

LOOK WE HAVE COMING TO DOVER!
TIPPOO SULTAN'S INCREDIBLE WHITE-MAN-EATING
TIGER-TOY MACHINE!!!
RAMAYANA: A RETELLING

British Museum

DALJIT NAGRA

FABER & FABER

First published in 2017
by Faber & Faber Ltd
Bloomsbury House
74–77 Great Russell Street
London WC1B 3DA

Typeset by Hamish Ironside
Printed in England by Martins the Printers, Berwick-upon-Tweed

A CIP record for this book is available from the British Library

ISBN 978–0–571–33373–8

10 9 8 7 6 5 4 3 2 1

Acknowledgements

Versions of the poems appeared in the following publications: *Battered Moons Pamphlet 2016*, *The Long White Thread of Words*, *Magma*, *New Boots and Pantisocracies*, *New Statesman*, *1914: Poetry Remembers*, *Poetry Review*, *Rialto*.

Some poems were commissioned by the following: Association of Creative Professionals, Bristol Festival of Ideas Utopia, Cambridge Thresholds Project, Mansio Project, 14–18 Now: Fierce Light Norwich Festival and Writers' Centre Norwich, Poetry Library 60th Anniversary, Southlands Arts Centre.

I am also grateful to my wife, Katherine, who is always my first reader; to Edward Doegar and Richard Scott for their illuminating insights and encouragement; and to my editor, Matthew Hollis, for his inspiration and for his guidance of the manuscript throughout its various stages.

Contents

BRITISH MUSEUM

Father of Only Daughters

Thousand times or more tonight
now you're in a big-girl bed
and it's mum's rare night out
I've simply flown upstairs

to watch you upside down again.
I'm so *oh* over my head
knowing you're safe at this stage
behind your bed-guard.

Two years old, already a clown,
you're the jumping sidekick
to your bigger sister
who's kicked off her duvet again.

In my past, I was treated
as a child when I was a man
and forced to remain in wedlock
to uphold the family name.

Look at me flying upstairs
on the wings of my shame
for my second-chance life.
A life under yours in a fall.

Vox Populi, Vox Dei

That he should opulently inherit
The goods and titles of the extinct.
– ROBERT GRAVES, 'A Country Mansion'

Who are we at root?
To know this is to know our range, the cast of characters
    we've banked?
Weren't we once a plucky bunch in battle led by Drake
    and Nelson?
Wherever we died turned Britain forever? An amphibious tribe
    who fished,
however far we ventured, our rivers coursed within us to chant
    our poetic names
roll on sweet Avon, sweet Ouse? The apple fell on Newton
    so we walk tall,
stay tall for Brunel and Darwin? Who'd speak for our garden
    utopias? Not Clive
of India, not Kitchener's finger, but John Barleycorn, the Green
    Man. Weren't we ruled
by black emperors? Our first couple of Obama glamour,
    Septimius Severus
and Julia? Who else to deepen us? Surely Julian of Norwich
    in her Albion
of divine love? The Tolpuddle Martyrs? What heritage or
    broch or crop of
skyline stone abounds us with murmurs of ancient wisdom?
    So much at root,
what ramparts of fear have we built? Have we been severed
    from the world?
Could we seek guidance from the Virgin Queen, the Lady
    of the Lamp,
so we're bold as Boudica, noble as Livingstone and Bevan?

Prayer for Gurdwara

They are domed to the fore through my Larkin train-brain
from as far afield as Glasgow, and glowed on
the hilly godliness of Huddersfield and Sheffield.
Tucked-in safe along lanes, their golden liquid nirvanas
bob on alabaster to nod a modest arrival.
So many of them in Birmingham and Southall,
my landmark temples. My satellites of Amritsar, bowed upon
each shul and church when an Almighty is in every heart.
Wherever our gurdwara song of universal brotherhood
is braided it's there we seek to beacon our land
and beckon indoors any wandering soul or Sikh, to impart:
you are lives upon lives in a drift through the weave
of consciousness, we honour you now
with our accordion choral songs and evergreen saag
and mild masala chana. Our sacred langars
from saffron evening to evening on the smoke off a stove
to stave off the feel of the end of home.

I am Sikh by birth, secular by nature,
when has our holy book ever hurt Britain?

Broadcasting House

Have I landed at the country of Truth?
          A regent battle ship of Portland Stone
             built between the wars. At the helm
its guide to the islands, Prospero,
defiant behind his flautist child of the air,
Ariel. Do we not, all of us, project a spectral self
          aboard a shared liner?
    Are we bound through the same arch
        to experience a communal voice?

I wear my lanyard about these halls
          to gauge our island pulse.
Are we at home in our sound, or are we moored to this
controlling vessel
with its daily middle-ground of worthiness?
    Are we set to the tune of an undertone
who aims to parade us beneath our Union Jack?

To cross the path is to enter All Souls Church:
        God's eye?
     Or is this, the final spire by Nash,
a face-off with our House? Its sepia columns
        remind us bells once sang from churches
    to host a heaven in our English ears.
Has a burden fallen to the hourly pips and the plum tones
of a crew who must bridge what seemed a commerce
       between the globe-as-one and our land in tidal retreat?

From above, along the hub of our vessel
                    are the flanks or shape of a craft.
Perhaps it's why this ship grew
                    from its art deco chambers
        and dark Tasmanian wood. Our vessel is modelled
for the new millennia: its ground floor decked
                    like a submarine dock with a facade
of glass and open floors around a column of light.
                    An inner atrium
where this light, with its daily illumination,
        shoots out for the sky, or is it being shot down
                    across each level to shorten
perspective?

    II

On the Ground Floor of our House hangs a tapestry,
                    a gift for services to the Resistance.
Within its woven bower, an amazed man who's merged
                    with the birds and the trees that surround him
                    with song and scent.
That image was inspired by Eluard's poem, 'Liberty'.
                    In the poem, the speaker wishes
                    freedom
            for the magic of night and the white page
and all the things besides. Uninvaded,

        have we been groomed too long by London,
by the rot of its sleazy core? Could Ambridge cleanse us
if the room's a squeeze for Black Country or Cornish?
        Is our House held to ransom by demands
                    from angry callers, or ministers,
                        who'd raise the roof to shout,

our House is too pro *this* or anti *that*:
Israel, Islam,
        chavs, Slavs, trans-gender, No Platform
        Policy, global warming, Charlie Hebdo and so on?

        Has our ship travelled far to come indoors?
Christmas at Fools and Horses,
seasonal dance-offs and celebs on sofa?

When did we lose our voice or, poles apart,
                a way to recover the centre?
Is our stance, our fussy pursuit of the facts, too grand
when heard against the homespun knowledge of chatrooms?
Should we grapple with rank ideals in public
                to blood the air between us? Has 'heated debate'
caused a knife wound
in our language? When the flag at the Palace weeps,
                say, for the death of a Saudi king,
                must our vessel, as dictated by the Houses
of Parliament, echo a voice of grief?
Could we risk
        our mike at the mouth of a source risen
                from its region?
At best, do we subvert with Book at Bedtime
        so our bed sheets might ruffle
        for Lady Chatterley's Lover?

Have we been knocking on doors again for a gift left us
                        by Uncle Sam? Now water-
boarding is all the rage,
how long can our House employ its greatest weapon:
                                the question?

III

There is a ship of man
that becomes a ship of the world in Piers Plowman.
There, the waters are Wealth
through which a vessel rides.
The fortune of a vessel lies within the rise and fall of the waves.
Our House is a vessel that's geared to sift
the waves, the fortune,
and so broadcasts the worldly profit and loss.
I watch a portion of this strain
from the building's upper floor, a United

Nations of tongues. One desk is all Bogota,
another is labelled Western
Central Asia on a deck that never sleeps.
From their channels they present an unvarnished
version of home to home.
Does our Service prove we're preserved in order
to signpost each dodgy Globocop, each demagogue?
To write the Bobby's report although the Bobby's under mask
and is filling his boots?

What of our own estate? How do we build a new being?
Could we update our failed and mural customs?
Become the Plowman who ascends the Hill of Battles
with ideals?
Could we shed Bias, armed with Knowledge,
Conscience, to fight for a steadfast voice?
And accept that to stay at sea is to stay at home?
And not bully for John Bull
or the teacake vistas of Betjeman? Straddle the centre
and not become anodyne?
To serve and be served by our House.

Inside and out along the piazza
our House is awash with the sounds of our island.
          An autopilot of accord and retort.
No longer replenished by ourselves,
as we diminish, or implode, are we doomed to look back?
Back at the dream that fell from the airwaves?
               This craft of the national mind? This Tower of Truth,
          this Roman Forum, this thoroughfare of modern Britain,
                    this gilded world,
               this happy field of people?

Cane

No English talk at home! my mother booms
in Punjabi. Our carpets bloom florals
from where she sobs at each Punjab film
when lovers croon along sugarcane fields.

I turn my head from her soppy Pollywood.
She cries that my tongue is sold on a language
that stole her life for the rootless exchange,
like sugar that travelled one way,

and offers to arrange me a wife and a cornershop;
when I steal off to study for an English degree
at our shop back door, she stands between us
to hold me firm, and sob, *No speak white girls.*

She's been here so long that I can't follow how
she won't ripen with time. Only when torn
does she meet my sweetheart, who bears
our roses. My mum blushes to say, *Berry kind.*

Our tongues are reined in: I keep my own counsel
and let the air go bitter when she won't sustain
Katherine. Once when she called, instead of *she,*
she said the name aloud. It was cut down to *Cane.*

Naugaja

Last millennium, the generations with plough and scythe
        were governed by the seasons and the local gods,
by a whole way of life bent at the knees
                in upraised prayer
        for the festivals of harvest, Holi and Diwali.
Each village enshrined in itself. So a trek over two rivers
        might sea-sicken the barefoot wanderer.

Yet from their landlocked acres they were the causeway
for the history of conquest. From Alexander to the Mughals
                till partition.
Through it all, the elders preached caste, the ordered rites
        where each kept in strict accord with each
        as dictated by the word of a bygone millennium.

Then the day men squinted from fields at a grain
                flickering shadows that rose towards a giant shape
        garnered upon the sky. What they saw aswim
                were the treasures of Lakshmi and her clouds become
                        golden coffers.
With glazed eyes they were swept along by the surge
        to find themselves in a far-off trove,
                the revolving haven of a foundry.
        It's here they swayed the flesh, that phantom,
hooked on the power of Time and Overtime.

        From the fidgets of a floorboard sleep they flew
on the indigo passport of the Crown so they'd pluck
the broad-shouldered goddess of their awed destiny.

They were eye in eye and rich as a rajah
carrying their maharani to the jasmine scents of their own
mahaal in the Motherland.
How easy it must seem, in the absence of a threshold
for humans to uproot and carry wholesale
their prophets of the air.
Their milk and cane of home that abides in the heart
undislodgeable.

Did any of them become household names? Whose image
limelighted the mind? Yet these uneducated tribesmen
were pioneers with their garlands and bhangra
for distant bale dreams.
Refashioning their corner shops,
their emporiums, luminous aisles and masala restaurants:
open doors every day across the facade of the Kingdom
that made them a frontier people.

What hurt them? One day, they watched their lineage
in a language gobbled as the native,
with the alien ways of the sports and the touchy-
feely dances.
Or saw their youth shawled inside a raw faith.

The preacher heard them say they'd laid their children
each week before the whirling incense of the Holy Book
for the far-off rituals, the habits.
So where was the soul of the village in their children?
Had the men severed the ancestral bloodline,
their women, under years of the Singer machine,
become bleary,
for this?

The preacher roused spells and potions.
Whatever the mantra from whichever new preacher,
        or the snake priest by the snake shrine,
        still their children could not
                be fathomed.
                Till the father,
                by the gas-work,
                on the way home
                from work,
                wept.
While the mother lay in the war bunker, in the mind that lay
    in the middle of the garden, and felt again the crossing
                malign her womb.

Were they really here? Were they the husk of a dream?
        Shadows who heard the ghost-force of the fathers
        on the sand-veranda calling them home?
Now one by one, in old age, they disappear.
We are their offspring. We watched them in their haunts.
I declare their earthy values, all they grafted on this soil
        with honest toil, with communal love,
                with the dignity of Jinnah and Gandhi
                are the enriched values of Britain.

Though our children do not speak the foreign tongue
        and though we pour mustard oil at the hearth
or do not wash our hair on a Thursday
                and uphold this or that dispensation,
                        may we raise ourselves to claim
                that a generation past with plough and scythe
        we were formed by the seasons and the local gods
in a primal village. A village my ancestors called
                Naugaja.

Hadrian's Wall

Around the old blown names
Birdoswald, Cawfields or Vindolanda,
each fortress and straight line of stone
partition was built by a zealous emperor
to keep out the barbarous.

I've come to this wall crowning England,
this symbol of divided man,
to honour the lineage of our tall ideals;
to ask, the more stacked, the more shielded
a haven, the cleaner the stock?

Where will our walls finally end? In
the gigabytes of our biometric online
lives, in our passports? To keep us
from trespass, will our walls be raised
watchful as the Great Firewall of China?

'Even when we weren't touching we were
making love'

is from 'The Balcony' by Louise Glück.
I feel I should say this to my wife.
It's too dramatically American
when our lives are afloat in a nervy comfort.
Enough to know, yes of course she'd pass the Glück
test when we're side by side chopping greens
or when she's away on a psychology conference.

Upstairs from my window I catch a woman
walking down the middle of our road.
I'm sure I see it more and more in Harrow.
Are these Romanians and Asians scared

an arm on the pavement might pull them in?
Who'd report the loss? What happened before
the crossing, or here, that leaves them exposed?
In the early hours, foxes fall from the sky
and pace along the dotted lines of our road
to cry like multiple girls: are these
women the silent day-version?

Do they bawl so quiet their eyes have left
the road that's turned ocean, turned into passage
where a car cannot pass them but turn them up
with their minds all the time on the one making love.

Philanthropy

That every way leads to
the wishing well.
On the *pluck*
and splash
of fallen change
Lakshmi will lay you
her yellow path.
Go now
be bold
for the task
of your dream.

He Do the Foreign Voices

. . . ah Weialalaah! you say in time with Eliot
as you head for the rubbish dump on Sunday morning
listening to your CD of those free rhythms
for *Mistah Kurtz – he dead,* for stranded Tiresias
     and Lil, for Krishna, for the *Datta*
        and *Da Da Da.*

It's now you feel most akin to Kamau Brathwaite
who, back in the day, implied it was the voice
     itself, not the words –
        the Eliot twang, the mock English –
that persuaded the empire's embrace for colonial verse.

With the windows down, the roof dissolves,
     you're swayed by the lazy turns but feel goaded.
The pile-up of white males in English anthologies
enriched the garden of your adult studies.
     Your like-minded friends regard the expense
        of verse a waste, an embarrassment.
They bypassed your dated muse
     to forge their forces on a Bhabha, Spivak,
        Žižek or whoever.

Out of the car, you're aside the other men now
    hurling down towards each labelled container
     as you land on the usual thought.
What comes of verse at the dawn of catastrophe?
     For the valleys smeared with murder
where somewhere just now a poet will be pulped,
in a state of terror,

verse seems redundant to cause – at best, an orison
or epitaph. An adult in kindergarten
        with a surplice song-and-dance
of decommissioned moods for the lyric graces.

You drive away, yet somehow affirmed,
more in love with your pretty airs
                that update the same old,
                that speak to power and fear,
whether they're heard or not, they'll say, head on,
        before family and blood and wealth
    our hoard of words must cleanse the world.

On Your 'A 1940 Memory'

Not one of your Somme poems,
yet Sassoon you'll end up there.
From a 1940 afternoon of war's
worst troubles, you're caught
by a clouded yellow butterfly.
You claim you're marked by it;
that its loveliness is a scorch
when suffering is everywhere.

The poem written years after
the morning you stalked a loitering
butterfly like a dream-hunter.
The freighted gain of each step
in a sunless mid-September
invokes in me your youthful ire
for the Somme's sunlit picture
of hell. No wonder you tell us
that Time will blur the pain.

Dear Jack, do you feel blurred?
Has war left you to recall itself?
You, with the soldier smithereens
at your arm, the Hun dispersed
by the kamikaze day that you sat
in their bunker to read sonnets,
and how you simply couldn't die.

No wonder, you're our haunted
hero. Perhaps an image of Britain,
whose kin made a killing in India,
who chases from his country
home a clouded yellow butterfly
that's gone off course to recover
a sunny afternoon of Empire.

The Vishnu of Wolverhampton

I always be Laxman the hobbler
who leave the open sewer, the lemon trees
        at India's independence
        for the sawmills of Kamloops
and onwards for the middle of the motherland.
        Till they joke how far a mere hobbler has
          stretch his legs
from one to the other end of the British world.
So what can it mean returning home?

Yet only yesterday I see a pink cloud lost
and though I never before
        I wave to it. I think it is my wife
      Padma who passed away a life ago.
      Padma come from the homeland
to check if I hang out my washing.
When I point to my handkerchiefs on the line
she is a beaming cloud with silk lining.

I always dream of the marriage night with Padma
      how we never before have met
how we're locked in our bedroom by the villagers
      and the young girls in bare feet
who are all huddled and listening from the veranda.
How I'm trying to stand up proper manlike
     but outside I feel is all one ear
even the jackal is quiet and ready to laugh.
      And my bride stay sitting
      on the side of our bed-to-be.

She is stick of bazaar-candy-pink,
from head to toe, I feel in my heart
she is pure, too pure.

And not very manlike am I
when I, when I drop my chaddar
                and out come sticking my
                legs, my hobbledehoy legs.
But my bride loosen her sari
        and calm as Mother India,
Come to bed husband. I will love your legs.
Your legs are now my legs.

And in our love-trying and chuckling
she understand why I start to cry. I cry I love so much
my father. To win a wife for his cursed son
he become a man on his knees
and when he come up from the begging ground
                he come up holding
                this Padma-jewel.

She is a goddess I swear for any Rajah
but is happy with only Laxman the hobbler.

        These days I am widow-white haired
        and all my family have passed away,
        cloud-cut for the monsoon mansions.
In my dreams of Vishnu
I am ready to leave this skin for other skins.

My friend Ramlochan say, *All gods is dead.*
        It always bastard rain.

I say, *My dear Ramlochan, you always coming up dry.*
        In the eyes of our partition peoples
        did we not have kismet of Rajahs?
Why you expect in Wolverhampton a heatwave?

Only this, I pray.
        On my last day, my peoples
will light my sandalwood pyre.
        From my flaming body at dawn
my soul is rise and rising become a pink cloud
        flying to India where my Padma
        is also a pink cloud hovering for me.

Just before our watering down into all-time waters,
        for a long-time-no-one-seeing-us moment,
above a bank-side, above a fork tree
where the gods once straighten a cripple child,
        Padma and I will come together.
                One double-big
                chumchum pink
                chuckling cloud.

The Museum of Archaeology and Anthropology in Cambridge

I am held apologetically in a seminar room.
This is the dawn of my days as a poet-in-residence
who has been commissioned to produce a poem.
My host furnishes me with an apple strudel slice.

Yesterday, my slice was one of many settled before
the prime minister of Fiji visiting his island's wares.
I overhear our tyrant was not exposed to the 'cannibal forks'.
But was most impressed by the kava bowl and whale

teeth whose curves he stroked with gloveless hands
before being won by a slice of the sweetest English apples.

From the Ambient Source

Approaching midnight and floating into the train
a silver-haired woman takes a seat, and from her bag
appears Heaney's *The Haw Lantern*.

She flicks his leaves with vacancy. I've had too many
pints of Heaneyken and smile at my feeble joke
while she settles somewhere near 'Clearances'.

It's propped so his verses starlight and populate
our underground. So her frailness seems unburdened
in a world where hope stands brave as Stormont.

I love the way his journey lifts the vexed mind
so we gain the vocation of peace his lines demand.
So we're uprooted, yet rooted, utterly humane.

A stop, and the woman must vanish. She hovers
at his airy *Haw*, as his lantern bearers wake me
filled with the sounds of his mud-haunted rhymes.

My life is replenished. Does he surge now he's gone?
I feel his heart through his meadow vowels, his words
from his island attachments wherever they please.

When he ploughs his Ireland, I see gourds and grains
sprout over the Raj. History becomes a raas, a roadmap
and texture of empire for nourishing grief with grace.

If he becomes my dream mentor, from beyond the tracks,
could he show me the way to dignify what we've buried?
That we merely host the train of accusative thought

from the angered outsider within. Could my mentor
guide me into gravitas, so we breach the divide
in ourselves for a shared commemoration:

the famines, the battles, our jurisprudence and chin-up?
I'd remain on the train of trains to never arrive,
ever aloft yet lowered and ready for Mossbawn.

Could we run through that again?

Sleeping in Lindau

From home, on your heels through Poland
for the Alps and over the side where darkness
has overdosed Bavaria, dear Czesław Miłosz,
you're wide awake at four in the morning
past Lake Constance. You're twenty today
in the summer of 1931, fresh out of the East
and gone to get your head round the infamous
West. What better place could test thought
than a heartland? You pace along the boats
that touch masts in the stormy lake, then on
through the streets for the sloping conifers
past a woken horse who clops on the asphalt.

On the borders of Lindau dawn descends
as you make your leafy bed in the breath
of the Black Forest. This feels like a trial run
and you seem at home. In the decades after
Stalin and Hitler, you'll dissect the swathes
of time to help you scope the murdered
modest ambitions of your peers. Forced
into exile you'll cross the distant waters,
like the waters of Lethe, to be washed up
in Berkeley, a stranger. Your verse, a foreign
tongue for decades unread. Yet you'll spend
each day at your desk to conquer oblivion.

Your verse, built on the reflex of love,
its lesson that whoever can face up to horror
and survive must be held by a vision at root.
In your case, you'll dream of a grandfather's
farm, its whitewashed granary and its vow
of a stream that flows past a dozing child
who's cradled by the sun. A primal vision
that firms you to suggest we can eradicate
our own chambers of hate for we are a big
people who can forgive. So we daily enter
a nuptial governed by the moon and the nut
shell and a berry harvest big as kind dreams.

Well it's suburbia in here from where I write.
Where the fight with history of your generation
ended with our noble claims for a vacuum of
values to shore us from the starved at our door.
I'd hear your message that those who'd find
worth in solace must engage with the eternal
theme of tragedy. So tonight, I'll pore through
your pines of ideals, while your snores translate
through the leaves of Lindau to rest in the whim
of my sheets. So you'll wake to write a battalion
of beautiful lines for the life you'd lose for those
who'd be lost to the grave for nobody listened.

Ode to England

There was a time on your island of the spires
when I was a child in the clouds with no inklings.
My fingers woven and raised to your language
which came from the cuckoo on our roof,
          over which my sounds
were the hollow of its Indian cousin,
                    the kokila.

England, your scrannel songs were greetings
from paperboy to whistling postman to bowler hat
who nodded to boiler suit. The clipped laughs
and mumbles I mimicked in the mirror: my head
          upright as a gentleman
to fake the high notes as *rawwraww*
                    or croak *fleurrrr*.

Even your fogs, your ogre trees gargling in
our garden would make me climb our slanted
coal-hole. My arms wide as the eagle of the gods,
Garuda, I'd jump down for the garden's midriff.
          For the mound under which
there was a bunker we lit
                    with cedar wood.

Was I invisible? I was gripped behind railings
for each devotional ball which the boys chased
with plunder cries. I'd swoon at the grownups
who rolled gloss bowls within high hedges.
           From each the orts of conquest
and loss propelling forth
                    tussocky clacks.

You were the sepia monarch of the world
who steered our canal, which I thought came off
the Himalayas and curved for a cannibal bourn.
The boats stroked by dangling leaves and steered
           by bare-chested, tattoo men
whose pipes smoked past
                    the factory whistle.

Oh England, I'm left to summon your golden days.
A brillig of bonbon and sherbet awnings for butcher,
baker, Lipton's; the lanes wafting Yorkshire puds
with gravy that called home Brownies and Cubs.
           While allotment dads knelt to pluck
like flowers the first green saag
                    of spring.

Though the sky was ever blue as a Hindu god,
my joys and desires were soon behind doors.
I'd double watching cartoons on the screen
that stilled on two words I knew were a spell
           I'd shape with my fingers,
before I learned to read
                    and read The End.

Commemorating Mr Kumar

Your car is a shrine with its dashboard stickers
for Siva and Brahma . . . Your wedding band twirls
unconscionably about the bone . . . I've returned
from my student job at Penguin's factory
where I empty bins. You tap your ring
on your living room window. You want me to
drive you in your car to Hillingdon Hospital.
I'm not insured but I like my sudden illicit lift
into manhood. You're a sixties immigrant
left off the waiting list like forgotten data.
A first generation Indian with a much too-thick
accent yet you're always upbeat as Micawber
though you keep palming your colostomy bag.
We're the only two Asian families in Yiewsley.
If I were thirsty would your wife fear to hand me
a glass of water, fear of being cursed? I think
I've enjoyed secretly knowing you're lower
caste. I'm glad I'm your clumsy chauffeur.

Days from now you would die. Forgotten man.
You are always in my heart, reviving smiles
for our drive in your Datsun. Or when I'd sneak
to yours for your tales like the one about a man
who becomes a bank manager on gaining a son.
I should have fought for you, and told the doctors
you'd five teenage daughters who'd be put out
to work earning their dowry, that your jolly Betsy
Trotwood of a wife'd roll over for the brokers.
After trading the house for shameless weddings,
what new grooms would sweep at her door?

Have you become the living overwhelmed
by the prospects of life? Is this why you curl
for the prayer-balm'd corner where it's Death
and the kismet hereafter? You'll wear a trademark
smile on show for your corpse as we'll walk
past it to call it a failed economic sacrifice.

I stall outside Emergency. Petrol floods the car.

The Look of Love

Fairenesse seene in th'outward shape
Is but th'inward beauties Ape
– THOMAS CAMPION

I

How strange your eyes transfix
on my sight despite our amorous
alliance; I'd say they seemingly
wince.
Your eyes shielding themselves
from my primal genes in faux pas.

II

Or this at least is the racial cut
by which I desire to adorn my vision
when I think I've been cut
by those of your local
hue;
I think they think I'm the ape in the room.

III

How unawares we can lurk
under a neighbour's skin-underbelly
and imagine their bloodline
at root barbarous.
I wonder what you see in me,
who you think I really am.

IV

How often I dream you have me
laid on a bed
to illuminate that complex of taste reducible
to the dawn of primate-time.
Then you dissect the deficiency
from my DNA.

V

Once I was *coloured* and you were
English.
Do we struggle decoding that popular
nurture? In our daily rounds
you are in the majority
so you are inscrutable.

VI

I must not measure myself
by the wealth of your heritage
which will never be imagined as mine.
So you remain the corrective,
the panopticon,
the unavoidable silent centre of attention

VII

I must not turn upon.
No wonder I remain an Englishman
who lights upon the booty,
the freckle-island flesh of your sands,
who watches from up a tree
yet never leaves the accruing hints

of dark print.

The Dream of Mr Bulram's English

I

From chalk face to the latest newfangled screen
I remain an English teacher before my shades-
of-the-globe teenagers. With a click I summon
imperishable lines from our island and from abroad
for their marriage between sense and mellifluous
sentence, for the way they've jazzed our lexicon.
My awesome role's to grade but also to inspire
each teen with a lust for our courtly vowels.

II

I pray they'll honour this tongue William dared
never to conquer, for who dare battle against
an autochthonous force. I hope to spin their minds
timeless with Chaucer, Donne, Keats and Byron,
with Tennyson and Browning, and lead them across
the spellbound shores of our tongue Shakespearean,
rousing oration into stately cadence till it one day
fight on the beaches in that tongue Churchillian.

III

If some students in the double lessons feel trapped,
if this tongue feels a curse, this flesh feels too solid
without, if this language feels ill-begot so its terms
cause shame. If we're still at sea with the whip-hand's
lashing tongue, if we're still at sea and the margin's
fading . . . How can we thrive in the West unless we hear,
for better or worse, the link with our distant ancestors?
This heartfelt Word, evermore, this shared tongue.

IV

Our ancestors took on the grand dreams of the King
James Bible and grafted the English canon. I respect
the hurt but we're now in the main, now that thought
in this tongue springs universal. I wish my students peace
in a word so dignity reign. I wish them Martin Luther
King's imposing marble mimicry and free speech
steering its own course through the ruling demesne
to imply this lingua franca has become our lineage.

V

Why live in a tongue you'd hurt – you'd mercenary
grab the rules to bend, as if the migrant past justified
an off-shore narrative of high-tech fast-talk portfolios . . .
If my class tread on water and arrive at the isthmus
of poetry they'll find they're enshrined in high art,
they've a stake worth the investment. So I bless them
the passion of Wordsworth who saved and saved
simply to behold a canvas-bound *Arabian Nights*.

GET OFF MY POEM WHITEY

oi get off my poem Pinky
your porky fingers lard my lean sheets

look at my darkie mug – my indie tag
do you think I could think in the same old English
you keep to your standard my standard's bastarded

your editors boast they elect by taste
if they like me they think I'm exotic
if they think I'm too English I'm a mimic
is it time for a fresh look Pasty Face
I can write with two heads
yet you groan on the head you get

this poem bows to Coconuts & Half-Castes
this poem bows to Farrakans & Hindutvas

for the brown-nose reviews
for the brown-nose rewards
the pink men poets are in bed with the pink men poets
the pink women poets are in bed with the pink women poets
I got no pinky I'm out on a limb
I got no pinky I'm out on a fat black limb

the ones won't stoop before the Union
of our Queen cos their passport's green
must they swamp our Blighty anthologies
to dampen our Uncle Tom-ti-Tom-tease

do you pass the Black Test
do you pass the Black Test
are you stumped by the balls of this poem
are you stumped by the spin of each line of this poem

is your holy word a Whitey canon
when I drool at your canon
I drool at your lowing herd centuries of verse
that famed an isle & spoke for an echelon
grafted by so many gorgeous clerics
diplomats, lords, academics
Etonians & door-knocking Tory petitioners
sponsored by monarchs & earls & slave owners

when I think of your canon do I think of your cannons
if I allude to your canon do I soil your canon
so why would you hold me in kindred terms

on MY biggest day the paper headlines
IMMIGRANT'S SON WINS FORWARD
I'd corner you all in a corner of Adlestrop
then call for support but there'll never be enough of us
& you say *I was never in The Guardian*

this poem bows to Wheatley Senghor Vyasa
this poem bows to Kolatkar Brooks Kalidasa
when this poem's no longer bow-wowing
watch it rise in salute to the stallion
black power of Sir Vidia & Sir Salman

do you pass the Black Test
do you pass the Black Test
do you care to be stumped by the names in this poem
do you care for the balls of each line of this poem
are my too-many googlies way off course
should I ball a few straight balls

the lovers in my rhymes are in love in their beds and bazaars
my lovers are in love and I'm in love with my lovers
must you flatten my lovers in your sheets
till they're text-book samples
of the multicultural or the postcolonial
so we're chutnified
so we're sitarised
to serve some light on Whitey

I've been ruled & parsed
now Caliban's my voice
where all I can do
is climb after Langston Hughes
from the crown of his Mountain of Race
from my niggardly force
I will roar the Truth

I'd rather be slimy Kim than Satan's Milton
I'd rather be Kamban than Paddy-bashing Spenser
I'd rather be Tippoo light-charging Tennyson
I'd rather be hanging-Pandey than Shakespeare

Ghazal

is the Habeas Corpus in the desert *Inshallah*
is the Human Rights Act and Abu Ghraib
calling cards for the ghazi desert *Inshallah*

does the Kaaba glow on the road to Raqqa
what swollen pass will these sandals tread
for the curse of Jerusalem *Inshallah*

why are my daughters in the desert O *Inshallah*
who picks the pen from the head so its flesh
harden to a text in muezzin cry *Inshallah*

does one man set himself alight when his Allah
is beheaded by another man's Allah
so all Arabia cry to the last *Inshallah*

Olivier's Othello

The invention of Race and its run on the blood.
A man teased from his skin then back into skin.
The switch executed on stage. This time Olivier
plays the man. Olivier whose Christian name
is surname to empire's swashbuckling generals.
He was destined to be the General. I'm convinced,
William, you distance the master from the Moor
so we hear of Othello amongst Anthropophagi
at which Olivier's blackface bares the exotic.
Your raw politics of ink when actors must vent
waves of iambs on a feral reek over the ages.
To pinnacle with leering Olivier on a parapet,
Goats and monkeys! So the darks of his bulbous
eyes roll upwards to play the sport of the hot
globe kept back. Aided by your, *[He] falls in
a trance.* Africa afloat on Arabian charms.

A version preserved by the National Theatre
of Great Britain, adored by Oscar nominations
must be fair-minded. Perhaps I should weigh
the finale in terms of Desdemona, white as
civilisation, being savoured, while snuffed,
by a nasty mass for her privileged ignorance?
Or admire Othello's proud speech, a savage
in dashing robes with a blade, the face-to-face
of hero and anti-hero, as he calmly exploits our
sound traditions? To martyr the Moor within
so we win our catharsis? As perverse, I reckon,

that Olivier, who'd persevered under polish,
now arises like a Deus ex Machina, in cahoots
with his Renaissance bard, to execute justice.
The curtain must fall for the white man's bow.

Have I misunderstood the play? If art begins
in dreams should I turn on the staged instigator?
Which is he, the poet's piercing aside – the devil?
Is he also the black man in his act of playing up,
or his guise – the idol who administers the shame?
Is the one who pulls the strings of horror least
rewarding? If he's the poster-boy for his cohort,
can he be hurt when a cause is fleshed by hurt?
Ah Swan of Avon, or are you the Upstart Crow,
you're always at play in my head. To leave me
irked by my applause when the dream lives on.

Aubade

Somewhere in the sunshine of the everlasting dawn
            from my airborne stance
I feel absorbed across the broad pavement.
                  Or am I dissolved in a voice
                  that can't sever from its verse.

Am I adrift in my heritage? To shadow the breath
of our dear Guru Nanak. To hear him chant
            his *om* that balms
the rivers of old India. I sense his aura
            hold the wounded over water
till they're healed.

In my suburbia, all around me,
the saffron trees are unearthly presences.
            They bow turn by turn
                  and seem to caress or bless
                  with breeze and gentle leaf
each wearied pedestrian.

Have I become so numbed by routine
and the reasoned life
            that flecks from my past would ascend
                  from within to raise my flesh
                  so it learns outright pain?
In my feeble conceits, am I haunted by obsessions
            and can't keep off the need to revive
                  the lost faith?
            My dire need to survive above the sphere.
The idea of the vision as practice charged into plenitude.

All that Sikhism charm from my childhood
      has me span the soul of Nanak
from Lahore to Harrow. His soul uprooting concrete
      so the nerves of the world are flexed
      and greened by the branches of his lungs.

His soul seems everywhere, guiding us to head
for the centre of this road
      where he has opened the earth
      so it spreads into a river gush.
Into which, are we being lifted by the trees?
Could Nanak's branch-arms haul us
      and wallow us in his equable waters,
         return us freed
         from the grief-ache?
So we're built to withstand the ruin of sense.

The Poetry Library at Southbank Centre

I am descended from the gasping lanes.
       Yet you gave me breath.
I pray you nurture those, who'd stream their lines
       through your measured volumes,
       who'd dare the bind.

The Calling

the night is abrim with the in-between children
they are summoning Mother India

take us back   take us back   take us back

but the Motherland is piping the old grief
I was down on my knees   on my knees

why did you run for the towers
where the treasures of my heart are hanged

the night is abrim with the in-between children
their heads are down and they cry

take us back   take us back   take us back

our songs are afresh with the plough and the oxen
the smell of open fires where the naan is crackling

and our roses are the roses of home

Shame

I still feel stuck on my ex.
    For an age of the drawn-out divorce
        her arrowed sighs made blood of my
           name. This way she kept in line
              with our tribe and survived her kismet
          as the victim. I rightly deserved to
      swallow my tongue on desertion
   that meant the voice, the body
of my wife lay bare.

                    I feel stuck on the day
                I came across her. She braved a
           Hello. Nothing broke forth except I recalled
      the barbs, being barred from our child.
The way she gave her heart to the sacrifice;
      the widow's martyrdom in whites
          for a halo of weeds, that weep:
              even your mother bows before
                me O boy of Death.

Meditations on the British Museum

Mirrors himself in the cases of pots, paces himself by marble lives,
Makes believe it was he that was the glory that was Rome . . .
– LOUIS MACNEICE, 'Museums'

I

I stand dead centre at the treasure core of our crowning jewels,
      our Great Court
and noble casket, a back street open-ended Bloomsbury bazaar
      where every marvel
migrant, in the four-wing three-floor stone, is guarded quaint.
Come bask in our show of travels abroad, in millennia of
civilisation and handiwork as conceived by our fair isle.

Look at our roof, each triangular pane uniquely sized to renew
      perspective. Our house
of colonnaded counter-thoughts where my propositions are jots
      amidst a meandering
crowd who extend dreams on a statue's nine lost body parts.
Could this be a court for stock-taking, a spare room to measure
by upheld mirror our own silk goods and grave ills, our ideals?

Step back, who decided our taste? How did our sovereign
      palate come to be
enlivened? Was it the native's gasp for each object that banked
      our praise?
Did resemblance to Rome, to Athens lay these goods far from
the native halo to a pressurised soil where walls are postponed
for an expanded space? Where visitors film all Mesopotamia

or on a bend snap a sphinx – the essence of Phoenicia.
        Each allegorical
or tantric form shorn of its origin and tribal worship lauds
        itself
before its mild god, the British Museum. Inside the dome
a copper dome that's embraced by a green-glass bridge,
its columns facing each café and kiosk. A museum as nation,

as a fragment of varnished Britannica: here are our classrooms
        from Bermuda to
Burma; here's Rhodes plotting red train lines to froth in steam
        a cheek of Africa;
or here, the peoples in shell ornaments, chiefs, rajahs, mounties,
every parrot and howdah'd elephant stooped before Victoria.
So in empire we're compatriots lit pure as Bendigo, El Dorado.

II

Bring out the kids from the segregated schools. See them enjoy
        a jawed lioness
carved at the neck of a savage, in gold leaf and lapis lazuli.
        A body engrossed
by horses' hooves, a charioteer who arrows a running Assyrian
with a vulture overhead. A nude goddess swaying her necklace
of skulls while seated on a corpse. Ogres, griffins, fire serpents,

manacles, gags and coins. A weaponised chair. Cemeteries
        of human bone.
They're emblazoned. Cleansed of a barbarous home from
        which they were bled.
Is each dancing massacre, each perverse beauty, on a plate
or vase, the work of Love designed to leave us mollified?
With our global leaders, oligarchs and moguls, we go soft

about these rooms, despite some visitors who pray or cower
        before a relic,
what voice stimulates them? Are they held by the glare
        of torture?
Was our gaze educated to swoon amid the exotic sublime?
I feel sent packing to read between the lines a Burmese Orwell,
a Woolf in workaday Ceylon and a canon of post-colonialists.

III

Mazed by these time-compacted rooms, I feel prompted
        for guidance
out of the comfort zone of our myth-kitty. I'd slip the radar
        of the panels
relaying the ossified exchange of pacts and gifts. I'd stand
each object in the dock, then, with my poetic grounding,
have it account for the applause awarded its opulence.

I'd uproot my nice day out, and sense who, today, deserves
        to be selflessly
offended. This bare-tooth mask of Quetzalcoatl was bestowed
        on a god:
Cortez. Does this mask dare us to face how paradise was lost?
To face Montezuma who was bowed before Cortez and forced
to witness from god's great Toledo sword an unprovoked

genocide. I recall my screen reporting common or garden
        rapes,
poisonings, dismemberments in our suburbia. Should I view
        each vile type
of mind grappled as the bog bodies corpsing the museum?
The bodies Heaney delved to evidence a turf of manoeuvre,
empathy. Or try to decode the spirit of Yeats's resurrection

where his singing bird of Byzantium, high on its golden bough,
     tweets to a grandee
news about an imminent agony by flame. Till I'm furrowed in
     hope on Homer's
Shield of Achilles, its folk tilling the singing fields. To find
lodged here, too, an aspect of Auden's grim Shield. And ask
how has the primal vision endured? Each man still works

his plot, then prays before the sun. How long will they alter
     after winter
so their tool blooms bullets, body-belts? The Shield between
     heraldic harvest and
the towering lands razed. So who rouses who for a higher
tree of Death? Surely their faith alone builds rooms of fresh
ruin? Like dissonance in Forster's Marabar Cave, what sound

booms from these nooks summoning each child to its Tora
     Bora dome,
where an ordinance drones: *home?* Is a Frankenstein fanatic
     for or against us
while it reconstructs each blood? Could the museum help inter
our old ideas of the outsider breeding amidst/within us terms
such as *infidel, insurgent, vigilance?* Is our world now plinth'd?

Now Prospero's surveillance hoards our every scripted quip
     for the island
of our interrogation. Here's a Ramayana statue of the demon
     Vibishana
who betrayed his own kin to side with Rama, the foe, purely
for moral profit. When factions conflict nowadays, whose facts
add up? Are today's Vibishanas Manning, Snowden, Assange?

IV

I look to leave, but feel the heat from a head with blank eyes,
    a frozen beard.
It's our father, pure-minded Plato. Didn't he argue for exile of
    musician, poet,
playwright and reveller? From the cave of his ideal state
human shadows perform eulogy and hymn alone. No wonder
I stand in the Reading Room to rebut the gods so I can voice

the best of our house. My gilded masters who sat here to model
    compassion
that rose through the oculus, who'd say now, which sanctioned
    invader leaves
each trove unguarded while it enshrines another oil giant?
Which dignified nation looks away despite each precious cargo
of slave and migrant being run overboard, while demigods

set themselves in stone? While each new zealot blows history
    to the laws
of commandment? Which victorious rebel ennobles the art of
    rubble
piled high as human death-pits? Lately Baghdad, Nimrud,
Bamiyan went viral with statues collapsing in slow motion
accompanied by a voice-over of euphoric prayer. Let's praise

the unconquerable climate of our cultures who find a portion
    of their own
safe in this fortress, in our sovereign values where Britain is
    guardian
of the legacy to ensure monumental mankind stay immemorial.
We're at home, albeit lost, while roaming among our kind
in Cuerdale, Yarlung, Shang, Ashanti, Aulong, Kush, Thule, Ur.